LEAD

LEAD

A GUIDE TO FOSTERING PERPETUAL LEADERSHIP

By Marvelous Marv Allen

What people are saying about . . .

"Marvelous Marv's latest book, *LEAD: A Guide to Fostering Perpetual Leadership* will motivate you to be the genuine and authentic leader you've always wanted to be. In this book, "Marvelous" doesn't just give you philosophies of leadership, but gives you the highest gift—himself."

Sam Chand, *Leadership Consultant and author of New Thinking—New Future (www.samchand.com)*

"*LEAD* is no ordinary book on leadership. In a time when leaders either hide behind their egos or crawl underneath rocks, this visionary book does not simply offer thoughtful leadership principles; it shares spiritual wisdom from a man of deep faith. Whether you are a budding learner or stagnant leader, page after page, you will feel as if Marvelous Marv himself is walking alongside you with an arm over your shoulder, giving you a pep talk, saying, "I believe in your destiny." This how-to guide will bless your life!"

Rev. Kenyatta R. Gilbert, Ph.D., *Professor of Homiletics, Howard University School of Divinity*

"In today's world, to be an effective leader, one must apply a holistic self - a personal commitment to grow your inner spirit, beliefs and behaviors, and to outwardly inspire others. LEAD is a must-read book to equip you with tools to achieve inspirational leadership. Marvin "Marvelous" Allen has given us the best gift possible - his full self! Yesterday's leadership tools are not enough for today. Throw away the old maps and re-tool yourself with LEAD to reach new territories."

Douglas Ash, *Business Executive, CIO, Transformation Leader, Managing Director*

"It is my great pleasure to give my endorsement of this wonderful guide to all leaders, potential leaders, or anyone with a true desire to take their life to a new level! The author, Marvin Allen, is very intentional with providing readers with tools that will improve our spiritual, professional, and personal lives as we go on this self-reflective journey.

As a leader, one of your most important attributes should be living your life in such a way that others actually desire to follow you. This guide will equip you to not merely hear what others around you are saying, but to truly listen so they will sense that you are generally concerned about their needs and desires. This relational quality is just one of many game-changing skills for anyone in any capacity of leadership. Get ready for a journey through this guide that will take your life, business, or church to a whole new realm of excellence and your desired destiny."

Dr. Chris Bowen, Founder of Living Faith
International Ministries, Executive Director
of Dream Releaser Coaching

For foreign and subsidiary rights, contact the author.

Afterwords by: Dr. Haywood Robinson III, Senior Pastor, The Peoples Community Baptist Church, Silver Springs, Maryland

ISBN: 9781950718283   1 2 3 4 5 6 7 8 9 10

Printed in the United States of America

Table of Contents

PREFACE

I started the journey of writing a book many years ago. I had just received a new promotion, and I was determined to rise to the position of CEO seat of a large Fortune 500 company. To capture my daily thoughts and experiences, I started a journal, with hopes that I would one day write a book about my journey to the top. I planned to title the book, "How to Break the Proverbial Glass Ceiling." Surrounded by leaders who inspired me, I felt confident that I was destined to do this.

The year was 2005. We'd just relocated to a new state, where I would lead a team that had been battered and torn in the past. It was my job to inspire hope, bring stability, and regain customer confidence. It was the perfect job. For several years, I captured what I felt was important in my experience on my phone or computer.

Some years later, my company began to reorganize. I began to see leaders depart, and grew closer to the ones near the top. As I saw these leaders' realities, I began to realize that the proverbial glass ceiling was not a place I actually wanted to go. Yes, I wanted money and toys…but not at the expense of lifting others or keeping my family intact. I lost focus, and I stopped my daily discipline of recording important moments. From what I could see, the people above the glass ceiling didn't have a life that I wanted.

As I began to deal with my own disillusionment, I realized my nonnegotiables and defined who I was. I was unapologetic about my desire to lift others and sacrifice for my family so they could stay together and protected. By this time, my father, mother, and one of three older sisters had passed away. My children were growing up, and time seemed to be passing quickly.

Now, I faced a new dilemma: how could I inspire others to break the ceiling that *I* no longer desired to break? I realized the glass ceiling was not a place that someone owned or had set up; nor was it a place someone had the ability to keep me from reaching. The glass ceiling is actually a metaphor; it's different for everyone. For minorities and for women, it has traditionally been seen as an elusive place with limited access, controlled by those with power. But as I got closer to it, I realized that the traditional understanding I had was not representative of the glass ceiling I now saw before me. My glass ceiling was more about letting go and letting God. It was at this moment that things began to change for me. I realized I had discovered a unique way of leading that I needed to share with others.

Through all this self-discovery, I've had the marvelous benefit of having my darling wife by my side. She has blessed me with 3 children: Briana, Monica, and Wayne, who have always honored their parents and continue to bring us joy and delight. In addition to my immediate family, my sisters, my brothers and sisters by marriage also offer me immense support.

Lastly, I recognize and thank my nieces, Joi Chaney and Chenise Williams, along with sister Genene Henley, for being my first proofreaders.

Let's begin exploring the principles and tools that will help you make the most of your leadership!

INTRODUCTION

Yes, this is another leadership guide. Yet it is going to be different from others you may have read. Why? Because of its style, the self-reflection it requires, and the principles it offers. This guide is intended to be conversational; it's not my intention or desire to write a textbook. I simply want to have a dialogue with you about leading. Therefore, sentences may begin with pronouns and end with verbs—or even conjunctions. At times, I'd like you to pause and self-reflect, so that you can recognize your own behaviors and personal leadership style.

I have read several great leadership, motivational, and relationship-building books. However, few of these meet the reader right where they are and offer practical development tools. This guide isn't long, but it shares principles I've discovered over a lifetime of leadership—at home, at church, and in business. They're principles you'll be able to remember and employ daily. In short, this is a guide meant to help anyone foster perpetual leadership.

This guide has had many false starts over the years since I retired. I often wondered why it was taking me so long. Then, as I posed that question to the only one who could answer, I received a profound answer: I kept trying to start this guide in my own strength, based on *my* knowledge, learning and experiences. But not until I yielded my will to the leading of the Holy Spirit did the words flow! I've always been a faith walker, but I hadn't committed this guide to God in faith. When I did that, everything started moving forward.

During this experience, I was reminded of a fundamental Christian principle found in the gospels. John 14:13-14 reads, "And whatever you ask in My name, that I will do, that the

Father may be glorified in the Son. If you ask anything in My name, I will do it." John 15:5 continues: "I am the vine, you are the branches. He who abides in Me, and I in him bears much fruit, for without Me you can do nothing." Lastly, Matthew 6:33 says, "But seek first the kingdom of God and His righteousness, and all these things shall be added to you."

These scriptures communicated the following to me: Don't bother to ask and seek for things in your own will, because you can't handle them alone. Seek the one true God— together, the two of you can handle anything.

The Three Focuses of This Guide

When used properly, this guide capitalizes on the adage "each one teach one," because it follows a leader-learner model. The leader is the one serving as the mentor or guide, and the learner is the one being led. This guide presents a process wherein someone can LEAD another on a journey that allows the follower to dream out loud and un-HIDE. It allows the leader to BUILD up the learner through accountability, as they become who they are destined to become.

These three facets, LEAD, un-HIDE, and BUILD, form the framework by which we'll learn how to become better leaders (and followers).

We'll begin by exploring the acronym LEAD. We LEAD others by:

A) **L**istening to them,

B) **E**xploring with them,

C) **A**ffirming them, and

D) Living your life such that they will **D**ecide to follow you.

I'm excited to start this discussion with you. Let's review some baselines before diving into the principles of LEADing.

LIFTING OTHERS

I don't know if you're reading this guide because you desire to become a leader, or if you're already a leader and want to grow. Either way, this principle is for you. Leaders are made, not born. You evolve into a leader when someone else is willing to follow you. Regardless of your socioeconomic status, gender, physical appearance, heritage or any other marker of identity, you must have someone following you in order to be a leader.

A common thread I've discovered throughout my rearing and professional career is that I've always had strong people of character lifting me. One pastor taught me that these relationships are "associational blessings." I believe he used that term because every one of these relationships was divinely inspired. Another important thing to note is that they were all initially fostered as the result of mutual friendships.

Look at your own relationships. How many can you list that started as a result of having a common acquaintance? By using this term, "associational blessings," my pastor was emphasizing that God is the architect of the relationships which had become such a blessing to me. These bonds helped me remain positive, regardless of my circumstances, and taught me to always look out for my fellow man. Now, don't get me wrong—I face everyday challenges; however, these associational blessings have shaped my life. They've become a cornerstone of who I am, and part of my living testimony. They're proof of how God lays out our steps.

Many years ago, I was listening to a cassette tape (for those of you who aren't as advanced in years as I am, a cassette tape is an audio recording format that was popular from the 1970s to the 1990s). Oftentimes, I would listen to music or audio recordings on different topics while traveling long distances, or on my daily commute to work. One of my favorite recordings was from a motivational speaker named Zig Ziglar.

Ziglar was a popular motivational speaker. He said something that changed my life forever, and I still carry it with me today: When I greet someone, I should be focused on uplifting them. Ziglar explained that few people truly listen to what you say when you first greet them. Think about your own interactions: How often do you hear people use the common greeting, "Hello! How are you?" Depending on where you grew up, you may have heard that a lot. A popular response and follow-up to that question is, "Fine, and you?" Based on my experience, these responses have become so common that most people aren't even listening to the response!

More than 20 years ago, I began the practice of responding to the greeting, "How are you?" with "Marvelous!" That response appears to be a natural play off of my first name, Marvin, and always seems to catch people off-guard. The reactions I've received have been memorable. Some people automatically think of a famous boxer named Marvelous Marvin Haggler. Many are shocked, and take the time to pause and smile. When someone asks how I'm doing, my response is, "Marvelous!" 99% of the time.

Because I'm known as a person of faith, some people ask if I'm just lying all the time. I mean, how can someone feel marvelous each and every time you greet them? To me, the question is not if I am lying (and I will address that in a moment); the real question is, why are we conditioned to assume that someone cannot be "marvelous" all the time? Does everyone have to be down, burdened, tired, overwhelmed, overly busy, or hopeless? I'll let you determine if I am lying in my response. Believe me, people wonder about this all the time; chances are, you are now wondering about it yourself.

I don't believe I am lying to anyone. You see, I choose my response in order to reflect the state of being that I desire, and to lift the countenance of the other individual. It's true that I don't always feel happy, excited, or interested. But when I think about the alternatives, and consider the fact that God that has shown me favor by allowing me to awaken another day, "Marvelous!" is the state in which I aspire to be. Upon making that declaration, I instantly transition into and emulate my "Marvelous" mantra: "I am marvelous! How are you?"

Let me tell you one of the funniest responses to this exchange that I received. This one gives me a laugh and challenges me to speak up more: Someone once responded, "Horrible? Did you say Horrible?" I don't know if that was prompted by my countenance, my enunciation, or their own emotional state. But the one thing that's become clear over the years is that people are not prepared to hear "marvelous" as a response; they're either waiting for something common or something negative. When this person asked if I'd said, "Horrible," I held eye contact and calmly said, "No, I said marvelous." Their response was, "Wow...I was about to ask you what was wrong; now I want to know why you are marvelous. I don't ever hear that!"

Now, a door is open. People smile and want to know more about me: why am I "marvelous"? Mission accomplished! I have an opportunity to lift their spirits and share something that makes them smile—maybe even something that helps them feel better about themselves. Ziglar explained that the first few people you greet every day will set the mood for your day. If you initially greet people who are negative, or have a downcast disposition, your positive vibe may fade quite a bit.

My wife, Charlene, will tell you that I don't solely strive to motivate those in my social and professional spheres— I also strive to motivate my family. When my daughters were starting grade school, I would run through the house in the morning, singing, "RISE and SHINE, GIVE GOD THE GLORY!" My oldest, Briana, would cover her ears and cry, "Dad, please stop!" (My wife would concur!) My younger daughter, Monica, would act it out with me, expressing, "Bring it on, Dad!" All I needed was her encouragement to keep it up. During this time, little did I know that my youngest child, Wayne, was taking it all in. He didn't respond like his older siblings, but he secretly modeled that behavior. Often, he can be heard singing around the house boldly and loud. Today he is in his senior year of college studying voice at Morehouse College. My objective was to always be excited about a new day, with its new mercies. I am thankful that my family understood that.

By now, you've hopefully figured out that there's a deeper purpose to my greeting. The word "marvelous" has been used so many times that, one day, I received an official award at work. I became known as Marvelous Marv instead of Marvin Allen. Some of my colleagues never really knew my legal name, but they knew I was the "Marvelous" guy. It's always funny when people realize that my real name is Marvin. They have no problem remembering it, and they assume that's why I say, "Marvelous". But that's okay; because regardless of how, why, or when I deliver this response, it really does lift people's spirits. It was George Washington Carver who said, "When you can do the common things of life in an uncommon way, you will command the attention of the world."

Looking back over my life, lifting others has been a consistent behavior for me. I remember learning poems in early grade school. One poem in particular has stuck with me; I use it almost every day. It's a quote by Stephen Grellet, a missionary, who said, "I shall pass through this world but once. Any good therefore that I can do or any kindness that I can show to any human being, let me do it now. Let me not defer or neglect it, for I shall not pass this way again." Lifting others is a core belief of mine—one that, thankfully, has been represented in my character and practice. The next time you hear someone ask you how you're doing, my story may make you pause and consider how to respond in order to lift them up.

I hope that, if nothing else, you've picked up on the fact that I take an interest in others. Sometimes, this investment causes me pain and disappointment. But even when it does, I'm better for it. Throughout my career and community involvement, many have unknowingly participated in following my LEAD principles. For those who took the time to get to know me, they see that I'm always encouraging others as well as LEADing them. So, let's continue our exploration of LEADing.

Self-Reflection Questions:

⇨ *Whom are you currently following? Who is lifting you higher?*

⇨ *Whom are you currently leading? How do you practically lift these individuals higher?*

⇨ *How does Marvin's response change your perspective on how we answer the question, "How are you?"*

Homework:

⇨ *Seek out one person to learn from and one person to lead. Reach out to both of these individuals this week, and start building (or strengthening) these relationships.*

⇨ *As a leader, the next time somebody asks you how you are, be sure to reflect for a moment, then answer authentically and in a manner that also lifts them.*

Practical Application Points:

⇨ *Leaders are made, not born. You evolve into a leader when someone else is willing to follow you.*

⇨ *When you greet someone, you should be focused on uplifting them.*

⇨ *"When you can do the common things of life in an uncommon way, you will command the attention of the world."— George Washington Carver*

TERMS & DEFINITIONS

Before we get into the specific principles of LEADing, let's be sure we're on the same page. Leading, according to Oxford Dictionary[1], is:

As a noun, *guidance*, especially in a spiritual context

As a verb, 1) *causing (a person or animal) to go with one* by holding them by the hand, a halter, a rope, etc., while moving forward. 2) *showing (someone or something) the way to a destination* by going in front of or beside them

Both the noun and verb definitions fit with what I am about to share. I find it interesting and unexpected that Oxford defines leading in a spiritual context; but it's right on point.

When leading, we form connections beyond the physical. These connections cause us to join with those we're leading—this is the spiritual connection I believe is described here. I don't know your background or beliefs; but I believe that we live in a physical *and* spiritual world. For those of us who believe we can exist in both, we know there is life after our physical bodies expire. I believe God put us here not only to praise Him, but to be in relationship with Him and with one another.

Think about it: He didn't need all of us to praise Him. In fact, since not everyone chooses to praise Him, He could have avoided being grieved by only creating one person, who would have no other choice but to give Him praise and worship. Instead, God created us with relationship in mind, and gave us dominion over the physical realm. God allowed Jesus to enter

---

1 https://en.oxforddictionaries.com/definition/leading

our realm as a baby; and later, He established a covering and comforter for us in the form of the Holy Spirit. Relationships have always been at the center of God's design for humanity. Leadership is more than a management necessity; when it's based on relationship, it is spiritual.

Look again at Oxford's definition of leading as a verb. The holding of hands or bringing someone along with a halter or harness are things we can easily visualize. But notice the word "forward" in the definition. I don't know if I agree that leading is always forward. I believe we can lead people forward *and* backwards. People often see leading in a positive light, maybe because of their desire for it to always be so; but we don't know if our leadership—or anyone else's—is forward or backwards until we see the result.

To unpack this idea further, consider the following. Have you ever been physically pulled in a direction that wasn't forward? If your answer is yes, you have been pulled backwards. If it's no, keep on living. We may not always be able to determine whether others will pull us forward or backwards when we form that initial spiritual bond; but regardless, I'd venture to say that, when we link up spiritually, it's with the desire to move forward. Don't fret if you've been pulled backwards, or have experienced a setback. Someone once said, "A setback is just a setup for a comeback."

The second part of Oxford's verb definition also fits my argument. It states that to lead is "to show (someone or something) the way to a destination by going in front of or beside them." My friends, this is a magic clause for me. In your leadership journey, this is exactly what you will be doing. At times, you will be in front of the people you are leading; at other times, you'll be beside them. If you live long enough, you may be blessed to have them lead *you*!

My concept of leadership is taking someone or something from one level to another. In addition, it's accepting responsibility for developing untapped capacity in people and systems. Leaders carry with them a confidence as they do this. I hope you see that leadership is not about the leader. Rather, it's about the people, or systems, the leaders impacts. Now, you may be thinking that a leader's role is, at times, to maintain the status quo. I would call that managing, not leading. Nevertheless, it is commonly accepted that leaders invoke desire and hope, both inwardly and outwardly.

Outside-In (Inward) Leading is what you traditionally see in the workplace. Everyone is led by the leader, who is the center of attention or focus. This leader sets the vision, and everyone follows it. I use the term Outside-In because the learner is being led from outside of themselves to achieve what the leader wants. If you don't follow, you risk not being a major contributor to the organization. This happens on teams all the time and, frankly, it's expected in corporate organizations (and even in some churches).

When I was in the large corporate environment, a clear golden rule was, *He who owns the gold rules.* I don't know who originally said it, but we all believed it and behaved accordingly. It was the leader's way or the highway. This model has its place; but that is not the type of leadership I'm exploring in the principle of LEADing. The principles I'm sharing will work in all environments, and will allow you to become a better leader.

Inside-Out (Outward) LEADing is taking the time to lead someone where *they* want to go. If you are not leading where they want to go, you have to ask yourself if you're truly leading. Inside-Out LEADing is leading outside of your own interests, biases, and thoughts. You're helping unlock the capacity of the learner. While potential is limited, capacity can increase over time, and is based on what God allows you to reach. As your faith and relationship with Him grow, your capacity grows. Remember, leaders are made, shaped, and taught. So, this Outward approach to leading can and should be used for succession planning, maturing children, or the birthing of business or ministry. We are unlocking the spirit within our followers by leading them to achieve what they feel is most important to their destinies.

My principles follow a Leader-Learner format. Traditionally, people consider the Leader to be the one with the most power. When you employ the Outward Leading techniques of LEAD, however, you gain power via influence—not from hierarchy or position. Using the power of influence, you ultimately allow the learner to make the appropriate decisions for their lives, instead of telling them what to do. I've found these techniques to be extremely impactful in my life, because I'm leading beyond what I can do—and, hopefully, beyond where I have been.

Before we dive deeper into my principles, I need to share why the word "perpetual" is used in the title. Maya Angelou once said, "I've learned that people will forget what you said, people will forget what you did, but people will never forget how you made them feel." Think about that for a moment. Consider how that saying might be true in your life. Can you recall a stranger in your past who treated you in an amazing way? They may not have explained why they did it. They may not have even gotten a chance to introduce themselves. But you can vividly remember what they did.

I can remember going to a National Football League game as a young man. It was a game in Washington, D.C., and my uncle was a season ticket holder. The National Anthem played, and I stood and placed my hand over my heart, and saluted at the end. To me, I didn't do anything special except for maybe the salute. Every day in grade school, we stood and said the pledge of allegiance, so this was not out of the ordinary to me. Well, soon after the game started, the concession man came around selling food: all the stuff kids want…hot dogs, soda, candy, and so on. Whoever came to our section selling concessions stopped beside us and said that someone sitting behind us had already paid for whatever we wanted. This lasted the whole game. At the end, we learned that he did this because I saluted. I never knew his name. But I remember what he did and how I felt.

Today, I often find myself recognizing unique things that people do. When I do, I try to bless them in some manner. Why? Because I know and remember the value of doing something special for others. These acts of kindness will last long after the initial gift or thought. Every time I do it, I am reminded of that game; and I hope the recipients of my act of kindness feel as thankful as I once did. That simple act will forever impact me, and I plan to keep repeating it. I hope that, when I do kind things for others, they also pay it forward and do kind things for someone else. This is what I mean by "perpetual." When you follow this guide, I believe someone will be so impacted by you that they will repeat these principles for others, thereby making it perpetual.

Now, let's go learn about these principles.

LISTENING

As you've probably realized by now, LEAD isn't just a word to me; it's also a powerful memory tool. This acronym makes it easy to remember, use, and apply my key principles. In fact, you may discover other words that help you lead more effectively as you learn these principles. I encourage you to make acronyms, or also use other helpful memory tools, in your journey towards understanding and implementation. Do whatever works best with your own leadership style. Let's unpack the LEAD acronym together.

The first step is something many of us rarely do well: Listening. Whether we're listening to the someone's greeting at the start of the day, or listening to an ongoing dialogue, it's is not something that comes naturally to most of us. Why? Our society is becoming more and more absorbed with ourselves. Many have abandoned the idea of "we." It's all about "I." People divorce because "*I* want to be happy, and my partner is not focused on my happiness." People vote because "*I* want the politician to do what is best for *me*." People steal because "*I* want something that *I* don't have but feel that *I* need, so *I* can just take it." We can't both win; *I* must defeat you.

Believe me, the "I" attitude is a tough thing to tame. I continually fight it myself— and sometimes fail at it. Still, I believe God created more than just one human so that we would be in relationship with one another. Therefore, the concept of "we" is important to Him. This is why listening is fundamentally important to leaders.

I recently finished my coaching certification through the Sam Chand Leadership Institute. Although very popular in executive settings today, the concept of coaching is one that many traditional channels don't understand. I've opted to adhere to Dr. Gary Collins' explanation of coaching. He says that coaching is a positive form of psychology which focuses on finding fulfillment, enhanced performance, team building, vision casting, career growth, and reaching one's goals and dreams. In coaching, people are enabled to set and reach goals while focusing on present and future possibilities, getting unstuck, and turning dreams into realities. Unlike mentoring, a coach and a client are equals who work together to bring about change. The best coaching is typically done with people who have training in skills such as listening, asking powerful questions, and encouraging others.[2] If listening is so important that it's the first skill in the coaching skill set, it only makes sense to have it be the first step in LEADing.

Dr. Sam Chand says that every person has the "need to be understood, the need to understand, the need to belong, and the need for hope."[3] That is powerful. Pause for a moment and reflect on how these statements reflect your own needs. Do you desire to understand, to be understood, to belong, and to find hope in your interactions with others? Even in this I-centric environment, our connection with each other is fundamentally important. Dr. Chand is not speaking of a physical connection. He is saying that, beyond the physical state, you are spiritually bound to others because we each need understanding, belonging, and hope. We can't have our needs met without learning how to listen. So listening is fundamentally important to the spiritual connection formed in leadership.

Listening is more than hearing words, however. It's a form of communication that involves words, body language, atten-

---

2   Gary R. Collins, *Christian Coaching: Helping Others Turn Potential into Reality* (USA: Nav Press, 2002), 16

3   Sam Chand: Dream Releaser Coaching Summit August 8, 2018

tiveness, and the capacity to resist "quick judgment." These are powerful communicative bonding agents. Yes, bonding agents! When we effectively listen, we are forming a bond—like glue. As time goes on and a relationship is built, these bonds strengthen.

Try this; go to a local gathering spot full of people. Without engaging anyone, listen to all the things and conversations you can hear. In this exercise, you are hearing, but not bonding. Now, take a moment to speak to someone. Try to start a conversation about a topic of your choice. Don't be a creep. I'm simply suggesting that you take a moment to engage in a friendly, polite conversation with someone in a non-intimidating manner. An example might be noticing someone in need (i.e. their coat falls on the floor, and you pick it up and give it back to them; or you notice someone who is distraught or sad, and you ask if you can help). When we take the time to notice and invest in others, we have a much better chance of starting a conversation.

If you are successful, and time permits, see where the conversation goes. While this might not always result in a tight bond, a connection happens more quickly than we often realize. When it happens, be engaged in truly listening to the other person—not just with your ears, but with your words, body language, and attentiveness. If those bonding agents aren't present, the conversation won't last. You may be hearing them; but if you aren't listening, they will know it before you do. Look at the chart[4] on page 30 to recap the differences between hearing and listening.

---

4 Chand Lesson 4 Track 1 Coaching Essentials Student Guide Lesson 4: Motivational Interviewing, pg 6

Hearing	Listening
Passive engagement	Active engagement
Physical	Relational
Involves ears and ability	Involves body–ears; mind–thoughts; and soul–will
Involuntary response	An intentional response to what you heard

Take the time to actively listen to people. When you do this, you form an invisible bond that allows you to speak truth into that person's life. It may not happen overnight; but give it time. It will happen.

When we show genuine interest in those we lead by taking the time to really listen, we also build a bridge of trust. Trust allows a bond to cure over time; that's why it hurts so much when it's broken. Someone once taught me that listening is a way of building intimacy ("into-me-see"). This is because a large part of intimacy is sharing the innermost parts of ourselves with another.[5] Be careful. When genuine, this kind of intimacy can lead to unintended consequences. It must be managed with appropriate and healthy boundaries.

Many great leaders have been derailed because they didn't know how to maintain boundaries. The details regarding how to do this well will be addressed in a future guide; for now, know that listening has the potential to be a powerful spiritual bonding agent. When we abuse it, or don't control it, we ultimately risk ruining the bonds we build.

---

5 Moore and Moore, Chapter 10, Radical Love, pg 255

In addition to listening involving words, body language, and attentiveness, I also mentioned that it requires "no judgement." Authentic listening doesn't consist of judging the person who's talking, because you don't know their story. Have you ever tried to share your feelings with someone, only to be told that you "can't" or "shouldn't" feel the way that you do? Doesn't that annoy you? It annoys me! You can't dictate someone else's feelings. You may not have intended to make them feel a certain way; but you can't tell them they don't feel the way they do. So don't interrupt people—not even to save time by predicting where their story is going. You will never truly know their story, or their feelings, unless you listen.

A push for urgency also hinders listening, and ultimately drives one to make premature assumptions. You see, listening takes time. It requires us to invest in someone besides ourselves. If we only listen to what's on the surface, we will never understand or hear the root of a person's heart.

For years, as a systems engineer, I designed, modeled, and tested systems. When a failure in a product or system occurred that received visibility and high-level pressure, I was sometimes called in to help discover why the failure had occurred. I would spend a lot of time trying to determine the root cause of the failure. I was good at it, not because I knew what to do, but because I was trained to stay calm and focus on the task at hand. I didn't allow the pressures of management (spending less time and money to get more done) to cause me to make premature conclusions.

Some of you may be familiar with a fish bone diagram. Imagine a fish bone that has a single spine with many auxiliary bones connected to the spine. For the fish to function properly, each auxiliary bone must function while staying connected to the center bone. Without the center bone, the auxiliary bones would not be connected, and the fish could not function as designed. When evaluating failure, a fish bone approach is useful. If we imagine the center bone as the bone that leads to the failure, we must examine all the smaller bones connected to it—they are all potential contributors to the failure. Depending on the number of contributors, it can take quite a lot of time to get to the root. That's why cars have so many sensors. Without these indicators, a mechanic could take forever diagnosing your vehicle when failures occur. Therefore, manufacturers have designed the host of sensors we have today, which hold data and provide information to help assess why something has failed (or is about to fail).

When we judge during a listening session, we draw premature conclusions. We stop listening because we're trying to figure things out, or to get our points in. I get it: why listen when you already know where it's going? You have things to do; places to go; people to see. The problem is, when we approach other's stories and feelings with that attitude, we aren't listening. How many times have we heard someone describe a problem about something and we jumped to the solution, only to find out we were off? Ultimately, we end up annoying the person—or at the very least, causing them to hesitate the next time they want to express something to us. This is what happens when we don't take time to listen because we're too eager to render a judgement, prognosis, or fix.

Look at how medicine has evolved over the years. Medicine is a practice. Doctors are still discovering the complexities of the human body. Sometimes they, too, are so quick to solve the problem and give hope that they render a premature diagnosis. As time goes by, and they learn more, they may narrow the diagnosis—or change it altogether. The more we watch and observe—the more we listen—the more we learn.

I hope I've successfully presented the truth that listening is the first important principle of leading. It must be active—it's more than words. Your words, body language, and attentiveness all play major roles in your effectiveness. When you listen well, you form a bond. This bond may allow you to speak into someone's life, or to invite them into yours. Most people will also allow their leader to speak into their lives.

Ultimately, leadership is not about position—it's about influence and forming bonds. I've had the opportunity to lead many people, not because I had a certain position, but simply because I had influence. I got that influence by learning how to listen – using my ears, words, body language, and attentiveness, with no judgement.

Self-Reflection Questions:

⇨ *Why do you think our current society struggles to listen well to others? In what ways might you personally struggle with listening?*

⇨ *Do you find yourself needing the four things Dr. Chand identifies—to understand, to be understood, to belong, and to hope? Which would you say is your strongest desire at this time in your life?*

⇨ *Have you ever experienced intimacy gone wrong: broken trust or a fractured relationship because someone failed to listen to or see you and your needs? What was that experience like?*

Homework:

⇨ *Throughout your regular routine, stop and listen to the people (and activity) around you. Take time to truly take everything in, without trying to speak into it at first. What do you notice that you may have missed before?*

⇨ *Point out something positive to a family member, coworker, or friend that you notice about them.*

Practical Application Points:

⇨ *"God created more than just one human so that we would be in relationship with each other. Therefore, the concept of "we" is important to Him."*

⇨ *"Every person has the need to be understood, the need to understand, the need to belong, and the need for hope."—Dr. Sam Chand*

⇨ *"When we show genuine interest in those we are leading by taking the time to really listen, we also build a bridge of trust, because we have formed a bond that has cured over time."*

EXPLORING

Exploring is the second LEAD principle, and is a direct follow-up to the first. As we listen, we must explore what we hear and help others to share more, so that they discover more about themselves. In other words, you want them talking out loud. This is another time-consuming aspect of Outward Leading. If you want to lead someone quickly and painlessly, then these principles may not be for you. I want you to lead with no regrets. I want you to lead so well that the person you're leading develops beyond simply being a duplicate of you. When you are leading this way, it's not about you; it's all about the one you're leading.

Besides being a husband, dad, and engineer, I am a Life Coach—and I love it! As a coach, I have learned the art of asking powerful questions—questions that cause people to explore their own understanding and find their own way to getting unstuck. Listening enables a coach to know which powerful questions may be impactful to their client. Now, I'm not suggesting that you need to be a life coach; but I am suggesting that you use this principle with those you lead. Let's examine this technique.

When was the last time you enjoyed a roller coaster ride? What makes these rides so thrilling? For me, it's the anticipation of the next turn or drop. If you can anticipate it, you can prepare your mind and body for what's coming, and take a little of the suspense out of the ride. When I can do this, I may want to squeal like a baby—but I can act like I'm in control. However, when I can't anticipate or see the next turn, my mind and body are caught off guard, and I'm given a rush of emotions. These surprises cause reactions inconsistent with my normal behavior and demeanor. However, it causes my inner child to come alive.

Being a grown man, I don't tend to release that inner child in an uncontrolled state. After all, it could be embarrassing, and cause shame if the wrong people exploit it. Shame or not, the inner child is real, and it's a part of who I am. Because I've tried to suppress it so much, I realize that I've probably robbed my children of seeing more of it, which may have robbed them of real connections and enjoyment when they were younger. Now that I'm older, I embrace that inner child, and often wish I'd shared it more in the past.

Why am I taking you on this roller coaster ride? It's because, when we explore, we help discover what's hidden deep within our learner's inner child. The art of asking powerful, open-ended questions related to what you've heard (listened to) will encourage the one you're leading to expound more upon those points. This isn't always easy. Sometimes, it causes an awkward silence. It may take some time to build the necessary rapport and trust. Nevertheless, you must trust the process, and stick with this principle.

When you explore with someone in this manner, you get them to go beneath the surface. If you haven't built that bridge of trust, your questions might elicit a sharp, "That's none of your business," or "I don't care to share." These questions may even result in silence. On the other hand, you may receive a response like, "Wow, I haven't really considered that yet; but…" When they get to this point, the two of you are on an adventure ride. Neither one of you knows, at that moment, where it will take you; but it causes the conversation to move beyond the superficial.

You must resist the temptation to interrupt this process by offering advice or answers from your own perspective. Simply ride with them, and enjoy it together. This exploration will cause them to talk out loud, if it's their normal nature to do so and they trust you. Conversely, it may cause them to be completely quiet. However, if you interrupt the talker or the silent one, it will mess up the ride on which you've embarked. Learn to explore by asking questions *and* waiting for them to answer. This ride may go on for hours, days, months, or even years. But if you're really interested in Outward Leading, you must keep the ride operable and serviced. Remember: it's not about you, it's about them.

Another important action to take while exploring is to write down mental notes of your learner's responses. This has benefits for each of you. For you, it helps you know what the next question might be, so you can go deeper and stay engaged. It's beneficial to your learner because you can repeat what they've said, which is a clear sign that you're listening. Have you ever had a conversation with someone in which you know you said something profound, but you can't remember what it was? I have, and it drives me crazy. When I'm talking to someone and they say, "Wow, it was profound when you said ...!" Their repetition helps me remember what I discovered.

Sometimes during these conversations, we have a difficulty remembering what we've said because we're not necessarily guarded or deliberate; we're simply having an authentic conversation. Now, let me reiterate that this kind of conversation may not happen in the beginning. As you listen and build trust, you will eventually witness this behavior. Why do you think this is? My non-psychology-degreed mind thinks it's because we become increasingly more familiar with the essence of another person the more time we spend with them. Your learner will be entering a place that most people never allow themselves to reach, let alone linger in. They will trust the one talking to them, and be okay with exposing information. In this deep place, you will find that there are several things that define a person. When you get your learner to this place, you are outwardly leading—helping them uncover their hopes, ideas, dreams, and excitement (unHIDE). Therefore, as you LEAD, the follower begins to unHIDE.

When we hear what a person is hiding, we find out who they are and what makes them tick. Reflect on your own past experiences. While in conversation with someone you trusted, have you ever gained additional insight you may not have considered before it came out of your mouth? It might have been hopeful—or painful. Either way, that information is part of who you are. It's at your core.

Why do you think getting people to this point is important in LEADing? So often, we try to lead people where *we* want them to go. I encourage you to resist that. I can't emphasize this enough: resist it even if the learner or follower is your child or successor. It's not about you. Don't limit another person by leading them where you want them to go (or where you've already been). That's Inward Leading. Do that only when it's about you, or you are trying to duplicate a process (i.e. running a restaurant chain).

However, if it's all about them, it's Outward leading. Help your learner to see beyond what even you can imagine. Get them to be the best *they* can be. Dr. Benjamin Mays said, "Do something so well that no man alive, dead or yet to be born, will do it any better." If you're leading another person, you want them to be the best at what they want to do. By exploring, you get the follower to unHIDE. When the follower unHIDEs, the sky is the limit; the cat is out of the bag; the train has left the station. Yes, these are all sayings I heard my parents or elders reference, but the fact is, you will have gotten them to a place that can springboard them to being greater if they're hiding hope, or assist them in getting help if they're hiding pain. You want the best for them.

I believe God put us here to be in relationship with one another. I also believe that our destinies—God's designed purposes for our lives—cannot be achieved in isolation.

Exploring can help one see their destiny. Notice two things about that statement: the first is that I used the word "destinies," plural. This is because God may repurpose us when we have shown that we are faithful (or unfaithful) to what He has asked us to do in any given season of our life.

I know what you might be thinking: Many of you, like me, have read books and heard speeches that imply we each have a single, solitary destiny. I'm not trying to discredit those authors or speakers. I think they're simply trying to convey that our destinies are the most important thing in any given season of life. Regardless of their intent, God has shown me in my own life (and in the lives of many others with whom I've had the pleasure to be associated) that we aren't limited to only one destiny or purpose; rather, we are limited to a single destiny or purpose in any given *season* of life. This is why it's not surprising that those who think they've achieved their life's purpose may venture off to pursue another burning desire or destiny, and achieve it, as well.

Simon T. Bailey, an author, consultant, coach, and former Disney executive, described purpose this way in a recent *SUCCESS* article:

> *We all want to live in what I call a universal assignment, the points at which your talents, skills, abilities and gifts intersect with a void or a need in the world around you. That is, as best I can imagine, the true definition of purpose we should all aspire to seek. But like anything else in the journey of success, it isn't a fixed point that you arrive at and stay forever. The world changes too often. We change too often. It is the constant search for that point that keeps us on target.[6]*

I've experienced what Simon describes; and I expect you may have, as well. Growing up, I always heard, "The rich get richer and the poor get poorer." It's easy to reproduce that which we already have. Too often, people assume that, since slavery was not within their lifetime or their parent's lifetime, that its effects on Blacks today in America shouldn't be a problem. That is far from the truth. I didn't grow up rich, and I didn't grow up poor; but I know people who are on both ends of the spectrum. In fact, if you ask those whom I knew as poor, they'd tell you I was rich. If you ask those whom I knew as rich, they'd tell you I was poor. I was neither rich nor poor in my eyes. I had and I had not; but I never went without.

As I look at these same people today, the resource spectrum for many of them hasn't changed. Is it all by choice? It's easy for some to conclude that; but I would argue that people's places on the spectrum don't change, primarily, because they don't understand or fully appreciate that oppression has a long-lasting impact. You can't just assume that a handful of

---

6 Success, What Is Your Purpose in Life, October 8, 2018 by Simon T. Bailey

programs will help a people overcome the lifelong effects of oppression.

Don't get me wrong: some of those who are resource-oppressed may break the cycle; but to achieve this, they must get rid of any oppression-induced behaviors and attitudes. They must see their lives from a position of victory instead of a pursuit of victory. That is not easy to do— especially when the world keeps kicking you while you're down. I am not offering any scientific evidence; I am simply offering a lived experience. It is much harder for poor people to become rich—and, conversely, for rich people to become poor.

When you start to LISTEN and EXPLORE, you may find people who already appear to be living their destiny who are willing to take on yet another challenge—or to admit that they haven't achieved what fulfills them. When people can do this, they've learned to live from a position of victory, instead of a pursuit of victory.

As a believer in Christ Jesus, I firmly believe I am fearfully and wonderfully made, as told in Psalm 139:14. Each of us has been perfectly formed according to God's design. Now, we don't all have the same physical or mental abilities. There are times when we struggle to understand birth defects and tragedies. But, our lack of understanding does not negate the fact that God is sovereign and shapes, or allows, our experiences in order to navigate us toward His will.

Spiritually, I am perfect in Christ Jesus according to His Word (1 Colossians 1:24). This tells me that I am victorious. The more I learn of God, and the more I tune my thoughts to His, the more I am convinced that He is mighty, loving, and purposeful. As I live in the victory He provides, I know that He will withhold no good thing from me. I've already been promised victory when I submit to His guidance and direction. So, if I am promised victory, I can live knowing it's mine. There's a song entitled, "What God Has For Me, It Is for Me" made famous by the Miami Mass Choir. This reminds me that what's been promised to me is mine as long as I believe it.

So the only question that's important about my victories is, "When they will happen?" This is a trait of many successful people: they know that what they seek is possible. They're not sure when it will happen. But their knowing drives them to keep pressing forward.

Destinies include or involve others. As an Outward Leader, you aren't living your destiny until you can ignite or start someone else on the path towards their own. This is especially the case in succession planning—when you find the right person to replace you in any position.

I often tell the following to people: "If you think a job or assignment is about you, just die, and you will learn that the assignment doesn't die with you." When I was a young leader in a corporation, a senior leader told me that my job was always to find my replacement. Some may think that this means I wasn't dedicated and committed to my responsibilities. That was never the case. I knew that my tasks were never about me; I was simply the steward of those tasks for the current season. The sooner I stewarded them well, the sooner I could get on to my next assignment, which was always leading me into another season.

When you LISTEN and EXPLORE, don't be surprised to see the things your learner unHIDEs, pushing them into a new season of life, even when they appear to have mastered the one they are in currently. God always has more for us to learn, do, grow in, and be in Him.

Self-Reflection Questions:

⇨ *Does exploring another person's thoughts and feelings intimidate you? On the flip side, do you find it difficult to open up to those who are leading you?*

⇨ *Think about a relationship in which you felt free to unHIDE and show your true self. What made the difference in these relationships for you? How can you offer those things to others?*

⇨ *Are you tempted to base your leadership of others off of what has worked for you? How can you practically begin to shift perspectives and discover what works best for those you're leading?*

Homework:

⇨ *Think of one to three people whom you lead right now or with whom you want to build a leadership relationship. For each person, write out a couple of open-ended questions that will help you explore who they are. See if you can work them into natural conversations with these individuals so that you can build a stronger bond.*

Practical Application Points:

⇨ *"When you are leading outwardly, it is not about you; it's all about the one you are leading."*

⇨ *"When we Explore, we help discover what's hidden deep within the learner's inner child."*

⇨ *"You may not be living your destiny until you can ignite or start someone else on the path to their destiny."*

AFFIRMING

The third principle of LEAD is Affirming. Often, when people consider the word "affirmation," the word "agreement" comes to mind. However, I want you to think beyond agreement, and consider affirmation to mean providing emotional and tactical encouragement. I don't believe you'll always agree with the path someone else is taking. I'm sure, as you look back over your past, you'll remember that it's difficult to get any kind of encouragement from people who don't agree with you. However, I'll reiterate that LEADing is not about you. You may not always agree with the path a learner is taking; but if you're leading them, you can encourage them to follow their uncovered hopes, ideas, dreams and expectations. Affirming them gives them the emotional encouragement to unHIDE what they have been concealing within themselves.

I'm sure you're cautious about accepting this approach at face value. One reason may be the fact that you can't affirm someone's desire if it goes against your own personal values and principles. While I understand this, I also think that we too often make judgements without truly understanding what the learner is sharing. Regardless, when you've invested the time to Listen and Explore with your learner, you'll have a better understanding of that individual's heart and thoughts. It's acceptable to share that you don't agree; however, it's more impactful if you allow them to *discover* that you don't agree by the way that you live and conduct yourself.

I got married at the age of 24. I remember my older sisters feeling that my wife and I were too young to marry. Both my future wife and I had just finished college, and were beginning our independent lives. My sisters felt we hadn't traveled enough or amassed enough wealth to get married. Still, while they didn't agree with my decision to ask my wife for her hand in marriage, they supported me, and gave me all the emotional and tactical encouragement I needed to live out my destiny. This year, we will celebrate more than 33 years of marriage. We've had more ups than downs, and God has sustained us throughout it all.

Another example of affirmation I remember occurred when I requested an intercompany transfer to a new start up division of my organization. This new group seemed well-funded, and had all the latest tools. I was so excited. I got selected for a job interview, and began to share my thoughts with the current leadership. They disagreed that it was a good role and fit for me, but they didn't stop me. After interviewing, I was selected, and began house hunting in the new location. My wife and I were having our first child, and we considered moving away from the support of family in Florida to a Southwestern environment, in which we knew no one.

My family was saying that this wasn't a good move. My current leadership at the time said so, as well. However, I was sure at the time that this was my destiny. So, everyone got behind my dreams and began to give us emotional and tactical support, despite the fact that they didn't agree with me. We kept moving forward, and tried to find my pregnant wife a doctor, and a house where we could establish roots.

As things were being finalized, our family began to accept the fact that we were leaving the area. One day, I got a request to meet with the company vice president, who presided over the group to which I reported. When I arrived, he had my request for transfer on his desk. He said, "Marvin, I am not going to approve your transfer. You're critical to a company capture we have going on at the moment. You can transfer after the capture is over."

I explained that my wife was seven months pregnant and that we wanted to get settled before the child came. He understood my rationale, and empathized with me, but he didn't change his mind. He did, however, give me an out: I could resign and accept the job I was offered; he simply wouldn't approve an intercompany transfer. He advised that I take the rest of the day off to think about my options. So that's what I did.

I got home and explained to my wife what had happened. I told her I needed to decide what to do next. As we talked, we realized that delaying the move might ultimately be better. By doing so, we'd be able to have the child near family. We could move later, after we got things a little more settled. Encouraged, we decided to stay where we were for the time being.

My wife successfully delivered our first child, and I continued to work on the company capture. My vice president got closer to me during this time. He watched how I behaved and stayed the course. He would often encourage me, and share what he saw in me. Ultimately, we didn't win the capture, and the vice president called me into his office again. He congratulated me on the birth of my child, and applauded my handling of the disappointing news he had shared months ago. He commended me on staying focused on the capture while being disappointed and upset. He then told me that my transfer was now being held up again.

Of course, I was confused. He clarified that the hold-up wasn't from him, but from corporate. It turns out that the group I was transferring to had lost all of their funding within their first six months, and the organization was being downsized. *Wow!* I was surprised and thankful all at the same time. Can you imagine what would have happened if we'd moved? I would have had a new baby in a new place, and been left with no job.

This story is a testament to our supporting cast, who never wavered. They encouraged us the whole time. They never agreed that transferring was a good move, but they also didn't stand in our way or try to deny our dreams. They simply journeyed alongside us, providing emotional support. Because my vice president had learned more about me and the potential within me, he began to shape experiences and assignments especially for me. This story is also a testament to our faith—to the fact that God always has us covered. We simply have to trust His process.

These stories demonstrate how you can encourage someone and disagree with them at the same time. You simply need to journey with them. It's fine to let them know that you don't agree; but it's not fine for you to stop giving them the emotional encouragement that allows them the freedom to unHIDE.

The emotional encouragement component of Affirming builds confidence and hope in someone. It keeps their hope alive. The learner can think, "*Finally*, someone receives and gets me!" Emotional encouragement supports our need for understanding and hope. This is essential in raising children, motivating others to go after their dreams, and helping people to overcome damaging words instilled by others.

Another characteristic of emotional encouragement is that it's designed to attack a lie. Using the word "lie" brings up strong emotions. I remember a manager telling me how proud he was of me when I was first hired as an engineer. I had done something outstanding in my role. While it has been some time, I can remember his words clearly. His intention was to congratulate me, but ultimately, he insulted me. I didn't know how to let him know how I felt, so I smiled and thanked him.

He'd said, "Marvin, you are different from other young Blacks. You are motivated, talented, and will be a great leader one day." I felt good and bad all at the same time. As I look back now, I wonder how many young blacks were told that they weren't motivated or talented— that they wouldn't amount to anything. Black men and women have listened to these messages— and, at times, accepted them because they came from someone in authority. But the authoritative message I received that day was a lie.

Telling lies is an easy way to discourage someone. It's a trick used too often. From a spiritual context, telling lies is always the goal of the evil one. John 8:44 (NIV) says: *44"You belong to your father, the devil, and you want to carry out your father's desires. He was a murderer from the beginning, not holding to the truth, for there is no truth in him. When he lies, he speaks his native language, for he is a liar and the father of lies."* and John 10:10 (NIV) says: *10 "The thief comes only to steal and kill and destroy; I have come that they may have life, and have it to the full."*

My manager was intending to encourage me; but when I look at those who look like me, and the impact this stereotype has had on many Black Americans, I get angry. I get angry because there are those who've believed these lies and perpetuated them, projecting them onto an entire race of people. Worse than that, there are those who've believed and internalized these lies as truths about themselves. Affirming uses the technique of emotional encouragement; however, be discerning as you listen for and target lies. Then, you'll truly help the learner to realize the lies they've subconsciously internalized.

Affirming allows a learner to hear words of affirmation that propel them towards healing and truth, so that their latter years can be their best. I've been blessed to have many people speak life into me. There's no better way to make someone feel understood than to encourage them in what they're saying. You don't have to agree with it; but you can't shut them down.

Look back in your life: what hopes, ideas, dreams, or expectations did you abandon because someone shut you down, or even failed to encourage you? Even now, you might wonder, *What if I had....?*

Hopefully, the shutdown worked to your benefit. But for some of us, this was not the case. Imagine being told that you can't achieve something you've dreamed of your entire life, simply because someone else thought it didn't make sense.

You may have heard it said like this: "You don't have the right background, race, money, or environment to do what you HIDE." So, you keep hiding it. Has that playbook been used in your past? Well, that's not the playbook of a leader. A leader encourages those they are Outwardly Leading, in order to capture what they HIDE and aid them in pursuing it. Then, the learner becomes free to take steps to unHIDE.

So much is forfeited because people fail to dream. Dr. Benjamin E. Mays says, "It must be borne in mind that the tragedy of life doesn't lie in not reaching your goal. The tragedy lies in having no goals to reach. It isn't a calamity to die with dreams unfulfilled, but it is a calamity not to dream. It is not a disgrace not to reach the stars, but it is a disgrace to have no stars to reach for. Not failure, but low aim is sin." Just because you don't see it, or can't envision it, doesn't mean it's not possible for someone else. As a leader, your goal is to get your learner to be the best they can be. Dr. Mays goes on to conclude the following: "Every man and woman is born into the world to do something unique and something distinctive and if he or she does not do it, it will never be done." Don't limit the ones you lead due to your own vision. Allow and encourage them to capture the essence of who, and what, is inside them.

You can tell that Dr. Mays' words are impactful to me. He is known for being a great orator and writer. When I met him, he was advanced in years and not very mobile. You had to get very close to hear him speak. Moments like these shaped a ministry function that I hold today: I am an armor bearer for my pastor. I have an appreciation for serving others that was birthed by examining the life of my father and other great men. God has sent me mentors throughout my life: Pastor Jethro Toomer, Pastor Hershel Palmer, Lee Norris Rayam, Rev. Jerome Brown, Chief James Wilson, Dr. Wendell Whalum, Lemuel Stallworth, Jerry Zionic, Pastor Alvin White Jr., and Pastor Haywood Robinson III. These men taught me about serving others, and helped me realize that, no matter the success I may have in my career, my greatest joys come when serving others.

Today, I live out my joy. If I had done this years ago, I may not have endured some of the things in my past (the good and the not so good). But, to God be the glory. He has taken my missteps, unbelief, disobedience, and lack of trust in Him and blessed me anyhow. Let's stop trying to measure success for others. In fact, I've embraced Booker T. Washington's definition of success. He said, "Success is to be measured not so much by the position that one has reached in life as by the obstacles which he has overcome." By affirming those we lead, we empower them to move one step closer to overcoming whatever obstacles might be in front of them. We get to help them in unlocking the power they have within themselves—power to press on. I don't know about you, but for me, that's a purpose worth living for.

The second aspect of Affirming is tactical support. This comes into play with the technique of accountability. Imagine what it feels like to finally have someone listen to you, explore with you, and emotionally encourage you. It's a great feeling! When we do this for others, we're promoting the art of self-efficacy. See, as we accept God, He allows the Holy Spirit to have a place of power within each of us. For those who are called His children, this power can be used on our behalf when we know how to tap into it. But merely knowing about the Holy Spirit is not enough.

We can all tap into the Spirit's power, but many will not be able to do it alone. I can't speak for everyone, but I don't believe anyone can do it on their own. I hear people tell others to pull themselves up by their own bootstraps; but all I see in this scenario is someone getting their boots on. They still need help and guidance for the direction they're going once they're suited up. So, what is needed besides emotional encouragement? Those we lead require tactical assistance; and that's called accountability.

Again, I remind you that being a leader takes time. Accountability helps those we lead to stay on track. When we finally get them to unHIDE, we can't simply leave them there. Now we need them to follow up and follow through. Remember when I said that what our learners unHIDE can either be positive or negative? Well, no matter the case, you need to ask questions to help them set goals and expectations for moving forward (if positive), or pausing to get help (if negative). You're still not telling them what to do. Rather, you're asking questions that help them unlock the power within to decide what the next steps may be.

Of course, you may ask their permission to offer guidance at times; but do this sparingly. Let them unlock their power instead of imposing yours upon them. If they want your guidance, the Spirit will prompt them to ask you for it. By following up and listening to what and how they're committing to pursue their path, you're helping them be accountable. This is a powerful step, because it's an action step. Everything else has been a step of searching. Now, your learner is moving.

This guide is evidence of this principle of accountability. How? I'd been saying since 2005 that I was going to write a book about leadership. For months and years, I kept a journal off and on. Despite one hard drive crash after another, I kept adding to it. I even started recording some audio on my phone. I was productive in gathering information, but I wasn't writing a thing. It didn't truly begin until my pastor asked me questions and pressed me about my answers. Then, I noticed others I trust also encouraging me to take action on what I wanted to do.

Still, the writing didn't start. Then, one day, I stopped, cleared my calendar, and started praying that God would help me get started. I came downstairs in my home to find a quiet place, and I began. I'd finally overcome what some call the "start-stop syndrome," which says that most people stop their breakthrough at the start by never starting. If it hadn't been for those who listened, explored what I wanted to achieve, and helped me by holding me accountable, I wouldn't have taken this step.

Is my Pastor a LEADer of mine? Yes, he is. Not because he imposes his thoughts, but because he listens, explores what I share, and holds me accountable for what the Spirit tells me to do.

Consider the three principles I've shared so far: Listening, Exploring, and Affirming. Do you have anyone in your life who's implementing these? Often, like me, many people do practice these things but don't see clearly what or why they're doing it…until someone takes the time to invest in them. If you have someone like this, take a moment right now to stop reading and simply let them know how much you appreciate them.

Self-Reflection Questions:

⇨ *Describe how considering affirmation as distinct from agreement might impact you. Who are some individuals with whom you may not agree, but whom you have the opportunity to encourage?*

⇨ *Reflect and consider how you received affirmation from someone who did not agree with you. Describe how that impacted you. In what ways did you benefit from it?*

⇨ *When have you ever been the recipient of an insult or lie buried inside of an apparent affirmation? Did this experience cause you to hesitate, double down, or even give up on pursuing your dreams?*

⇨ *Who are your current accountability partners? To whom are you an accountability partner?*

Homework:

⇨ *Choose one to three people whom you either lead or would like to begin leading. Think about ways you can affirm them, even if you don't agree with all of their decisions. Make a short list of affirmations for each person.*

⇨ *No one can do life all on their own. Think of one or two accountability partners—trustworthy, safe people who can push you towards your dreams and goals. Reach out to these people and ask them about their goals, as well, to see if they would be willing to partner with you.*

Practical Application Points:

⇨ *"You may not always agree with the path that someone you are leading is taking. But if you are leading them you can encourage them along their journey."*

⇨ *"There is no better way to make someone feel understood more clearly than to encourage them in what they are saying."*

⇨ *"Being a leader takes time. Accountability helps those we lead to stay on track."*

DECIDING

The last principle of LEAD is truly fundamental. Unlike the other three, this step is not initiated by the leader. That's what makes this principle so simple, complete, and unlike other leadership tips you've probably encountered. The last principle is Deciding. Perhaps, on the surface, this seems strange; so let's expound. Deciding allows LEADing to encompass a 360-degree approach by putting the burden on both the learner and leader. In this step, the learner makes the decision to follow the leader. Because it's the learner making this decision, he or she ensures that the leader never has to wonder if the one they're leading is invested; it becomes evident in their participation with, depth of discussion with, and trust of the leader.

Earlier, I described a leader as someone who can identify those who are following them. When the learner makes this decision, the process becomes circular and repeatable. You may wonder what this process looks like physically. In my experience, it has taken on various forms; but the most notable has been when I, as the learner, share with my leader the detailed steps I'm taking to follow my dreams. This level of transparency is evident, because no longer does the leader have to pull out information from me. Instead, I find myself sharing private details without prompting.

My most recent example of Deciding came during the time this guide was being birthed. After being led to unHIDE, I began to share with my pastor specific steps I was taking to turn the things we discussed from a dream into a reality. He wasn't telling me what do. Frankly, he didn't have time. I found myself eager to share, because I was excited, and knew without a doubt that my pastor was invested in me. He'd already led me to unHIDE things others had previously squashed. Having these discussions allowed me to be vulnerable without becoming fearful, because of the person with whom I was sharing.

This time would be different, because my leader was intent on building me up. The BUILD process is done by:

- **B**onding with the leader, so that the learner embraces the beauty in themselves and in others. The learner becomes bolder as they get out of their comfort zone and begin to help, or LEAD, someone else.

- **U**niting with the leader as the learner gets, and remains, unstuck. This act creates a win-win. The leader wins because of the great joy that results from walking with someone while they achieve their hopes, ideas, dreams, and expectations.

- **I**nvesting, as the leader shows why interdependence is important. We can't achieve our best alone. We need relationship and involvement with others.

- **L**ifting others up. We learn to show love by focusing on the needs and concerns of others. Encouraging others allows them to build confidence, and the courage to take risks as they learn.

- **D**eveloping as a result of the process by which we help others grow. The leader sets the learner on a path towards their destiny. We empower them with self-efficacy, because we allow them to see how they've unlocked things from deep inside themselves; they are empowered to find their voice and press towards their goals.

This BUILD process allows the leader to further inspire the learner as their relationship grows. Consider this thought that I once found and modified from an unknown online source: If you look at the people in your circle of influence and don't get inspired by them, you are encircled by a cage.

Think about the times in your own life when you decided to follow someone. What compelled you to follow those people? Was it because you felt they were inclined to support or invest in you? Was it because you had an existing trust built with them? Was it because they appeared to be successful? Was it because they had been places you want to experience? Was it because you were taking networking to a more intimate level? Regardless of why you made the decision, you probably saw benefits for yourself in following them. As a result, it was easier for you to accept their criticism, correction, and probing questions as they led you.

Now, think about mentors someone else assigned to you. What relationship do (or did) you have with these individuals? Were they truly invested in you, or simply to that person who assigned them to you? Many organizations use mentoring in their development programs; some of these initiatives are more successful than others. I can recall being assigned mentors at various points in my professional career. The functionality of these mentee/mentor relationships was evident; but in some of them, we never truly bonded enough to have genuine conversations that benefitted either of us. In fact, looking at the list of strong men who've played a role in my life, none of them were assigned to me by anyone else.

As a leader, you can listen, explore, and be affirming; however, if your learner doesn't make the decision to follow you, the leadership transition will not occur. I'm not saying that benefits won't result for the learner; but they won't become a leader.

Just imagine if more of us were doing leadership this way: How might suicides decrease? How might bullying decrease? By using LEAD, we can change the world by lifting one person at a time and promoting perpetual leadership.

At the beginning, I told you that I don't believe leaders are born; I believe they are made, shaped, or taught. You see, it's easy to tell people what to do. But until they can start achieving those elusive victories in their own lives, they will never understand themselves. According to ELITE-CV, a career branding company, 98% of people die without fulfilling their goals and dreams.[7] Obviously, there are several contributing factors to this statistic. I believe it's more than about not having a plan.

Although the burden in Deciding is on the learner, the leader has challenges, as well. The first challenge for the leader is to be someone worthy of following. This is where your walk is important. Few people intentionally choose to follow a dishonorable person (though many do it every day). We have a small group that meets in our home. When we were being trained to host the small group, we were constantly warned to be aware of how we live at home. This is because we were bringing people into the inside. Imagine if they found my home to be inconsistent with what they see on Sundays, or whenever I am around those of faith. If my wife and I were

---

7   https://www.elite-cv.com/blog/why-only-2-of-people-become-successful/

one way in public, yet another way at home, do you think those within my small group would stay under my leadership?

Today, the news is flooded with stories about those in ministry who have abused children in their past. I occasionally run into people that say that, if I had known this or that about them, I could have never followed them. Well, I make no excuse for those who have abused anyone; but I know even my best deeds are as filthy rags before God. I am sharing all this because, even when we follow someone, we often don't know everything about them. However, if we know they aren't honorable, we probably won't allow them to LEAD us.

So leaders, let's take time to invest in others. At no time should we allow or encourage them to think we are more than sinners ourselves, who need to seek God's guidance daily—by God's grace, we are saved and set free from the bondage of sin. Still, as Luke 9:23 reminds us, we must take up our cross daily and follow Him.

Another challenge leaders must overcome is a lack of self-confidence. Most people don't always feel worthy to lead others— especially when we examine our own secret flaws. Lack of self-confidence can cause a leader not to allow the follower to make their own decision. Why? Because the leader covertly sabotages the opportunity. I would remind each leader that, if they get this opportunity, they shouldn't shy away from it because of self-doubt. Instead of leading others to follow *your* thoughts, we serve our followers better when we help them deliver what's been birthed inside of *them*. This step will be a pivotal moment for the both the leader and learner. Both of you were created for such a time as this. Don't allow fear to paralyze either of you.

In short, making the decision to follow someone is the responsibility of those who are being led. The follower must make this decision on their own. This is the only way they will truly feel empowered.

Self-Reflection Questions:

⇨ *In what ways have you shared with someone the detailed steps you are taking to follow your dreams? Explain how making a concrete decision to detail those steps to someone affected your motivation to move forward.*

⇨ *BUILDing others up involves bonding, uniting, investing, lifting, and developing. Describe which of these comes most naturally to you, and how. Describe which of these you need to work on the most, and how.*

⇨ *Marvin writes, "The first challenge for the leader is to be worthy of following." What do you need to work on personally to become, and remain, a person worth following?*

Homework:

⇨ *Revisit the acronym for BUILD on pages 37 and 38. Choose one of the practices to focus on, and think of one person you can bond with, unite with, invest in, lift up, or develop. What are practical ways you can go about doing so?*

⇨ *Think of one area of personal development that you want to work on in order to become and remain a leader worth following. What resources and people can you reach out to for help in your development?*

Practical Application Points:

⇨ *"BUILDing another leader up is accomplished by bonding, uniting, investing, lifting, and developing them."*

⇨ *As a leader, you can try to listen, explore, and be affirming, but if the learner doesn't make the decision to follow you as the leader, then the leadership transition will not occur."*

⇨ *"By using LEAD, we can change the world by lifting one person at a time and promote perpetual leadership."*

AFTERWORD

So, what kind of LEADer are you? What kind of LEADer have you been? What kind of LEADer are you becoming? It seems that, in every field of interest, resources abound that claim to possess the "winning" formula, strategy, system, or steps for success. What Marvin offers here is the real deal. It's been my pastoral privilege to witness firsthand the power of this approach within his family, among his professional colleagues, and in the lives of many of our ministry staff, leaders and disciples.

Several things stand out about this model. First, it's very personal—and that's where true LEADership begins, isn't it? Rather than starting with the rigid formality of a position or title, it begins as an intentional connection of two authentic "persons."

The conversational flow of the book reflects and projects the quality LEADer most people desperately need in their lives. We all need listeners, explorers, and affirmers shepherding us along life's way. Imagine the carnage and wreckage made of so many lives over the centuries, which could have had much more favorable outcomes if only people knew that LEADership is possible without LORDship. Marvin extols "relating to others" above "ruling over others"—"guiding" above "governing"— "escorting" above "exhorting."

This paradigm is not only personal; it is practical, as well. From my limited observations, the steps outlined herein are used by ordinary people every day—individually, but not interdependently (an important distinctive of this plan). Something seems to happen in the human psyche when we are entrusted with a modicum of authority. As a new parent, teacher, manager, coach, elder sibling, legislator, and so on, too often we're prone to abandon these salient characteristics: Listen—Explore—Affirm. Perhaps it's in the quest to prove ourselves "the" LEADer that we inadvertently preempt the learner's choice to "decide" to follow us and, consequently, prevent true LEADership from being realized.

Beyond personal and practical, what you've just consumed, my friend, is proven. This is not mere theory. Real-life examples, from history and the author's own life, fill these pages, bearing witness to the extensive power of the principles. I am sure that in your family, during your academic journey, throughout your career, or in your present ministry or service, you can visualize one or more persons whose application of these principles contributed to the influence and success they've enjoyed. What greater proof do we need than Jesus, the Master teacher, who illustrated these LEADership qualities, as Marvin has highlighted throughout his work?

Lastly, how "marvelous" to have at our fingertips a winning strategy that not only is personal, practical, and proven, but is downright portable. There's no team, organization, community, family, school, or business where the LEAD approach will not yield improved execution, efficiency, and overall effectiveness.

So, my friend, you've read the material. What's your next move? Allow me to suggest that you re-read it…again and again. With each reading, use a different lens from one of the several influential roles you are privileged and ordained to occupy. Be sure to answer the questions and complete the assignments throughout.

Solicit a sojourner to travel with you. Journal as you journey. The notes will serve as mile markers, offering inspiration for you and future pilgrims you'll be blessed to impact. Surely, we'll continue to encounter people who could use assistance UnHIDEing—excavating their hidden hopes, veiled visions, and discarded dreams.

As this easy-to-read, easy-to-understand, and easy-to apply system begins to transform your life and LEADership, be sure to spread the wealth: Quote it! Post it! Recommend it! Give it away! Already, I can hear the next reader saying, "Thank you . . . I love it!"

Dr. Haywood A. Robinson, III
Senior Pastor, The People's Community Baptist Church
Silver Spring, Maryland

SUMMARY

LEAD—Listening, Exploring, Affirming, and Deciding. When you begin to use these four principles in your leadership, you are Outward Leading in a manner that is giving of yourself and making a difference—one person at a time. You have become more interested in "we" than "I." Some may wonder how to do this on a larger scale. To answer this question, I must refer to what I call "ground truth," and that is the Holy Scriptures. History clearly shows that Jesus impacted the world. Although He was holy in human form, He left a great example for us of how to make an impact: He started with twelve people.

If you run an organization, you can't personally spend this type of time with the entire organization. However, if those you LEAD follow your style, they, in turn, will LEAD others. That's how the multitude is led. Don't ever think you have to do it on your own—that's the trap of the enemy. Remember, to accomplish the great things in life, we need divine intervention and human relationships. You can't do it alone.

In the **Listening** section, you were reminded that, in general, many of us are poor listeners. When we do listen, we are using a form of communication that involves words, body language, attentiveness, and the capacity to resist "quick judgement."

In **Exploring,** you learned that the biggest tool in your arsenal as a leader is a proper use of follow-up questions that provoke your learner to unHIDE. This isn't a quick process; it can take days or years. It requires trust, and it looks unique in every leader-learner relationship.

I shared that **Affirming** must result in emotional and tactical support for the learner, instead of merely agreement. Helping someone finally understand what they're trying to express builds them up. As a leader, you may not fundamentally agree with your learner. Nevertheless, we learned that, in this step, the learner develops self-efficacy, confidence, and hope. It's amazing what can happen when people truly believe in themselves; that's why the learner must believe that their hopes, ideas, dreams, and expectations are possible.

Finally, LEADing a personal journey, and it requires the learner to do something: they must **Decide** to follow. The leader must commit, as well—both to boundaries and to doing their best to maintain a character worthy of following. Yes, the learner sounds a lot like the disciples of Jesus's day: they didn't know where they were going, but they knew Jesus was worth following.

What might happen in your inner circle if you chose to LEAD this way? Whose life could you impact? In the end, how much money we amass or how many things we conquer won't matter. However, the lives we impact will forever leave a legacy.

I believe in the Lord Jesus Christ. I believe He lived, died, and ascended into Heaven for me. I believe that, one day, He is coming back for me, and I will give an account for those I led and those I didn't. I once heard Pastor Mark Batterson share that, during his first sermon, he asked a group of elderly people what their biggest regrets were as they looked back over their lives. They unanimously responded that, "They didn't regret doing the things they did, but they did regret not doing the things they should have."

Remember to help those you lead unHIDE, so they will not look back and regret not reaching for the hopes, ideas, dreams, and expectations inside of them. When you do this, you are giving yourself to help them unHIDE and, prayerfully, live with no regrets. Then, we can truly say we are leaders who know how to LEAD.

Self-Reflection/Coaching Questions:

⇨ *Which of the four strategies in LEAD do you find most helpful in your leadership journey right now? Explain why you think you chose that one.*

⇨ *You have made notes about a good number of people in past chapters. If you had to narrow those people down to one or two persons you feel called to connect with on a deeper level, who might they be, and why?*

⇨ *Explain your definition of the follow terms in your own words:*

LEAD

UnHIDE

BUILD

Homework:

⇨ *Reach out to the people you chose and begin to build a stronger bond with them. See if these people are interested in having you LEAD them, and if they think you would be a good accountability partner to help them reach their dreams. Remember, don't pressure them, but let them know you're interested in who they are and in being a part of their life!*

Practical Application/Takeaway Points:

⇨ *"Remember, to accomplish the great things in life, we need divine intervention and human relationship. You can't do it alone."*

⇨ *"It's amazing what can happen when people really believe in themselves."*

⇨ *"In the end, how much money we amass or how many things we have conquered will not matter. But lives we have impacted will forever leave a legacy."*

DECISION TIME

Thank you for reading this guide. I pray it has made you think, and realize how LEADing can help you change the life of someone else by helping them find success. Since you got this far, let's not stop. Take some time to think of someone you can LEAD. I'd love to hear about your progress. I call this section "Decision Time," because I don't want this to be a guide that's bought and simply put on the shelf. God birthed this out of me in order to be shared. I've used the principles of LEAD to teach in corporate America, in discipleship circles, in success planning, and in personal mentoring. It wasn't always easy or convenient; but in the end, it's always been beneficial.

Have you ever attended a seminar or a training that you thought was outstanding? Can you recall making some type of statement of intent or commitment—an action step you were going to take based on what you learned? Were you disciplined enough to follow through with it? Or did you allow life's circumstances to get in the way and prevent you from implementing what you learned? How can you prevent the latter from happening this time, as you finish this guide? Go back to the homework assignment in the Summary and answer the following:

⇨ *How soon are you going reach out to each person (hint: select a time and date for each one)? What is your best strategy for ensuring that you hold to that commitment (calendar entry, task entry, telling someone else, etc.)? Whatever method or strategy you chose, take a moment to document this step now, and record the commitment so that you are held accountable to it.*

⇨ *What specific approach will you use with each person? Why do you think the approach(es) you chose are best for each person? How do you plan to make them feel that your LEADing journey is more important for them than for you?*

Now, it's your turn to go forth and LEAD!

SAMPLE USES

LEAD is flexible, and can be used in various ways. I have found it very effective in ministry, marriage, and management. The key is having both a leader and learner with the desire and time to commit to each other.

LEAD in Ministry

It's not only natural for leaders to help other leaders; it is a God-given responsibility for disciples. Geiger and Peck suggested in their book, *Designed to LEAD* (p. 64) that the leadership God has entrusted to us can be categorized as follows:

- Leaders are called to reflect God's glory.

- Leaders are called to replicate.

- Leaders are called to cultivate.

Using LEAD, we reflect God's glory by giving hope. No matter where you are on the continuum of faith, hope is a by-product of faith. We are not Jesus, and we can't save the world; but we can use Jesus's approach and give hope, one individual at a time. LEAD does just that.

Death is a fact of life. We may eventually cure cancer, stop car accidents, or perform plastic surgeries to hide the appearance of age. But ultimately, we will die. When that happens, I believe our ability to influence others doesn't end— if we've employed the perpetual leadership principles of LEAD. These principles allow you to consider those who come into your life, instead of merely focusing on your own circumstances. Remember, we are placed here to be in relationship. We need each other. Let's not squander these connections.

As leaders, we know we're still sinners. Yet, I pray that, as a result of our faith, we sin less. How can we replicate righteous behavior? One way is to allow others to get close to us so they can see how we follow Christ. This is the hidden power of small groups. When we watch people on Sundays, we form ideas and thoughts about who they are; but when we get an opportunity to have closer relationships that allow intimacy (into-me-see), we learn that they are similar to us. I truly believe that young people shy away from traditional churches because these churches don't tend to encourage authenticity. I'm not advocating for sin to be tolerated; rather, I'm advocating for us to remind everyone that we are not perfect like Jesus, so we must take up our cross daily and follow Him. Jesus led his twelve disciples to change the world. When He returned to heaven, he left us with the Holy Spirit to guide us in our daily walk. Now, he sits at the right hand of the Father to advocate on our behalf. We may not change the whole world, but we can influence a few people, like Jesus did with His disciples.

As we replicate our walks as disciples, we are cultivating the lives of others for the glory of God. We must be hope-givers, and let this dying world know that, through Christ, all things are possible. Not some things, but all things. Not just little things, but all things. Not just big things, but all things. Our hopes, ideas, dreams, and expectations are possible through Christ!

I believe there are light and dark forces at play in our world. Both attempt to influence us. Whichever force we listen to will guide our behavior. We must know our Master's voice. We are not immune to sin; but if we've accepted Christ, our souls have a home when we die. As we replicate our walks and team up with others to provide accountability and we produce other hope-givers like us.

LEAD in Marriage

My wife and I lead a marriage ministry in our local church. I tell people that we do this because she has me in remedial training. So I get to practice over and over how to be a better husband while I share with others. One of the greatest tricks of the evil one is to get us isolated—to make a couple think they're the only ones with the issues they're experiencing. If you're married, you know what I mean. Let's look at some examples of these issues:

- You make money, but you're constantly more broke than you'd like.

- You feel like you've lost your identity.

- At first, your spouse made you happy; but now they don't, or you do not feel happy enough.

- Your sex life is okay, but it's nothing like you had imagined.

- You consider "what if" scenarios far more often than you should.

- Your spouse doesn't seem to meet your needs.

- Your spouse doesn't talk to or share with you.

- Your single friends envy what you have; and, at times, you envy what they have.

- Your spouse doesn't see what you do for them. You give, give, and give, but it's not noticed.

- Your spouse isn't as attractive to you as they used to be.

I don't know your story; but after 30 years of marriage, I know that your story is not unique. We've used LEAD to help couples communicate what's truly going on beneath the surface, and what they desire most. Too often, one spouse tries to invalidate the other's feelings. One thing we've learned is that you can't negate someone's feelings. It may not be your intent for them to feel the way they do, but you can't tell them that what they're feeling isn't real.

We don't want other couples to have the marriage we have; we want them to have the marriage God intended for *them* to have. So, using a concept from *Radical Love*, we remind them that, "Your Spouse Is Not Your Problem, Your Sin Is Your Problem" (YSNYP, YSIYP)[8]. It's all about perspective.

LEAD In Management

Today, with the rapid advances in technology, the work-force is constantly changing. It has become more distributed; we're moving away from doing business in large factories and plants. When I retired, I had weeks of vacation I hadn't used. I look at my children's practices, and know they will not have that problem. They take time off from their jobs as often as possible. They work from home as much as possible—nothing like what I did in my prime. Leaders can't effectively lead via fear anymore. They must lead with influence.

Young people today are more interested in their quality of life than their rate of pay. They've learned that quality of life has a higher priority. LEAD allows you to build trust and relationships so that you can be a leader with influence. Your team may not be near you, but this will help you know what's on their minds and hearts. When you do this, you'll find that they give you their best in return. In this guide, I mentioned succession planning. LEAD is perfect for accomplishing this, because it helps you bring out the best in your successors, so that your impact will outlast your years.

---

8 Moore and Moore, Radical Love

CPSIA information can be obtained
at www.ICGtesting.com
Printed in the USA
FSHW020803240620

9 781950 718283